Paper Tiger
An imprint of Dragon's World
Dragon's World Ltd, Limpsfield, Surrey, RH8 0DY, Great Britain

First published by Dragon's World Ltd 1994

All the illustrations in this miniature edition are from
Chiaroscuro by Tim White published by Dragon's World Ltd

The catalogue record for this book is available from the British
Library

ISBN 1 85028 275 7

Editor: Julie Davis
Designer: Megra Mitchell
Art Director: John Strange
Editorial Director: Pippa Rubinstein

Printed in Hong Kong

TIM WHITE

PAPER TIGER MINIATURES

magination is our
pathway to change.
Without the ability to
imagine we would be
trapped — trapped in
what we term reality.

ut then our reality, the environment we live in, is actually the end-product of imagination.

uch of what assaults our
five senses was once
a figment of somebody
else's imagination.

All the major innovations, those things we now take for granted and which affect every facet of our daily lives, were once contained in the single thought, What if...?

he zenith of technical achievement must surely be the android: impervious to the ravages of time, stronger, more intelligent, superior to man in almost every way.

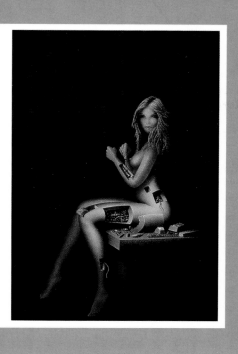

he progressive
evolution of robots
poses a question
regarding the future of
artificial intelligence
that is perhaps a little
disturbing.

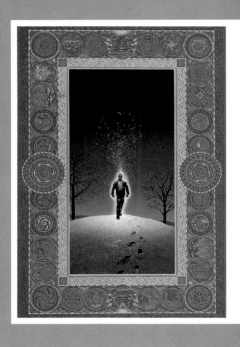

e has taken over a
human body which
can scarcely contain
his immense energy.
He is a primal,
rudimentary force, a
kind of destroying
angel blindly seeking
out his victims.

eath is but a link in
the endless chain of
life, death and rebirth,
a door from this world
to the next.

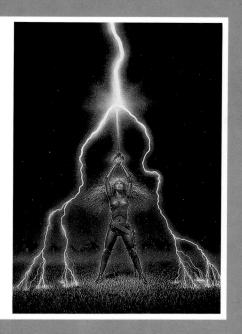

he idea of a fairyland
is so much part of our
culture that its origin
is difficult to trace.

re fairies elementals? Spirits of the dead? An extinct race remembered only in stories passed down through the generations? Or are they simply a product of man's vivid imagination?

ne belief is that fairies are fallen angels, not good enough for heaven and not wicked enough for hell.

herever they fell they stayed: in the air, on the earth and underground, inhabiting streams and rivers, trees and flowers.

hough generally helpful
and nourishing, like
nature itself these
elementals can be
dangerous if treated
with disrespect.

any of the taboos and superstitions that abound in fairy folklore are related to people's fears of fairy magic and their wish to protect themselves.

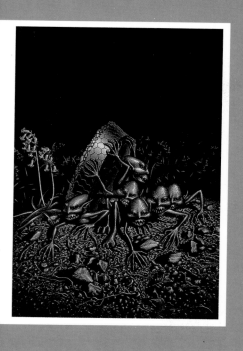

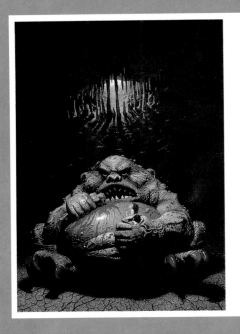

ome fairies are of decidely nasty character and there are accounts of fairyland that describe it as a highly unpleasant place.

n contrast to those familiar figures which have their roots in folklore, there are certain elements which have filtered through from the horror genre and actually achieved a kind of mythological status.

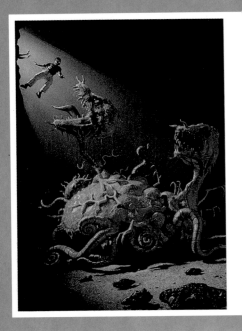

t is possible that these mythological creatures are manifestations of our unconscious fears.

he danger lingers on. They lurk in subterranean caverns, beneath the vast wastes of the Antarctic and out among the stars.

belief in aliens is virtually a social taboo. But looking realistically at Earth's relationship to the rest of the universe the odds are stacked high in favour of there being intelligent life elsewhere in the galaxy.

ooking up at a star-sprinkled sky and realizing that each one of them is a sun like our own evokes the same kind of awe and wonder that was once inspired by the mysterious unexplored regions of the Earth.

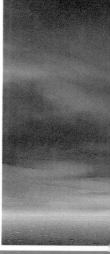

MANIFEST DESTINY